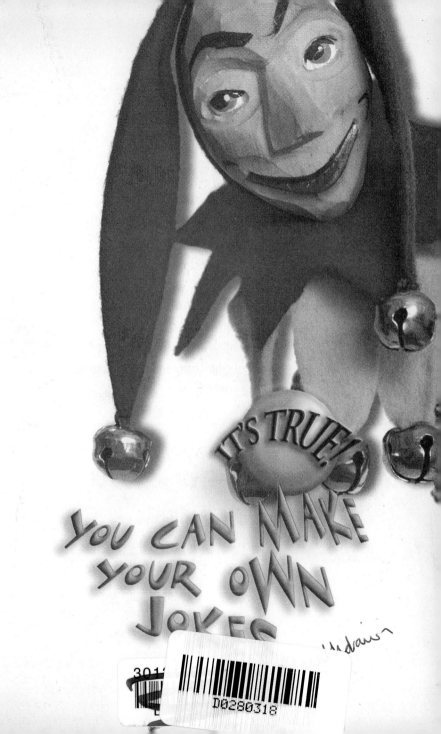

IT'S TRUE!

YOU CAN MAKE YOUR OWN JOKES

Did you know that frogs are cannibals,
fashion can be fatal and the dinosaurs
never died? Or that redheads were
once burned at the stake as witches?
Find out why rubbish tips are like lasagna,
and how maggots help solve crimes!

Books to make
your brain bulge!
find out all about them on
www.itstrue.com.au

Sharon Holt

PICTURES BY Ross Kinnaird

IT'S TRUE!

YOU CAN MAKE YOUR OWN JOKES

ALLEN&UNWIN

For Alan, Gregory and Sophie,

who keep me smiling.

First published in 2006

Allen & Unwin
83 Alexander Street
Crows Nest NSW 2065
Australia
Phone: (61 2) 8425 0100
Fax: (61 2) 9906 2218
Email: info@allenandunwin.com
Web: www.allenandunwin.com

National Library of Australia
Cataloguing-in-Publication entry:

Holt, Sharon.
It's true! : you can make your own jokes.
Bibliography.
Includes index.
For children aged 8–12 years.
ISBN 978 174114 733 9.

1. Wit and humour, Juvenile. 2. Comedy – Juvenile literature.
I. Kinnaird, Ross. II. Title. (Series : It's true! ; 21)
808.7

Series, cover and text design by Ruth Grüner
Cover photographs: Getty Images (man)
and Bob Elsdale/Getty Images (pigs)
Set in 12.5pt Minion by Ruth Grüner
Printed by McPherson's Printing Group

5 7 9 10 8 6 4

**Teaching notes for the It's True! series are available
on the website: www.itstrue.com.au**

CONTENTS

CHEEP JOKES

WHY JOKES?

My nine-year-old son loves making up jokes. He used to tell really BAD jokes that weren't funny because they didn't have a punchline.

Knock knock. Who's there? Dinosaur. Dinosaur who? Just dinosaur. See what I mean?

One day when I couldn't stand it any more I sat down to explain to him how jokes work. I've always loved listening to jokes, but I'd never been very good at telling them. We came up with some simple instructions for different types of jokes, and within days we were writing dozens of original gags. Like this one . . .

Knock knock. Who's there? Dinosaur. Dinosaur who? Dino-saur you were home so we thought we'd drop in.

That got me thinking about humour in general. I did some research into clowns, riddles and April Fools' Day. I wondered if laughter really was the best medicine. And of course I wrote more jokes.

Me, a joke writer? You've got to be joking! But if I can do it, so can you. Have fun!

1

JUST JOKING

Q: What holds a microphone and clucks?

A: A chicken singing karaoke.

Q: What's the quickest way to the hairdresser?

A: Take the short cut.

Q: Why do French
people eat snails?
A: Because they don't
like fast food.

Q: Why did the mermaid close her eyes?

A: Because the sea weed.

Q: Why was the hen disappointed?
A: Because she counted her chickens before they were hatched.

Q: Why did the three little pigs leave home?
A: Because they lived in a pig sty.

Q: What did the fly say when the bee asked it out on a date?
A: Buzz off!

Imagine a world without laughter. No jokes. No clowns. No farting cushions. Sounds boring, doesn't it? What's more, having a good sense of humour helps us to stay well, fight illness and live longer. Some researchers believe the human race wouldn't have lasted without a good giggle every now and then. Maybe it wasn't survival of the fittest but survival of the funniest! Let's face it, we were born to laugh. We even have a funny bone!

THE TRUTH ABOUT FUNNY BONES

Sorry, folks. The funny bone is not a bone.
And anyone who's knocked their so-called
'funny bone' will know it's not even funny.
It's actually a nerve called the ulnar nerve
which runs down the inside of your elbow.
If you knock that part of your elbow
against something hard, the ulnar
nerve gets trapped against the long
bone between your elbow and shoulder.
That can cause a strange tingling feeling.
The term 'funny bone' probably came about
because the long bone running down to the elbow is
called the humerus. Humerus, humorous – get it?

THE FIRST JOKE BOOK

Have you ever wondered who told the first joke?
One of the first joke books, or jest books as they
were originally called, was written by a Greek funny
man named Hierocles, possibly in about 500 CE.

Ancient Greek and Roman comedies also made fun of everyday life, and joking is even mentioned in the Bible. Jest books were all the rage in Europe in the Middle Ages, when times were tough and a good chuckle helped lift the mood after a particularly gruesome series of battles and executions.

BRAIN BENDER

When you listen to a joke, your brain reacts as though it is hearing a realistic story. As the words unfold, your mind expects a sensible outcome. When the end of the joke is different to what you were expecting, you laugh. It's the brain's way of coping with a sudden change.

THE WORLD'S FUNNIEST JOKE

The world's funniest yolk

An Internet experiment from September 2001 to October 2002 invited people to email their favourite jokes. More than 40 000 jokes were collected and people voted for the funniest. Two million votes later, this was the winner:

Two hunters are out in the woods when one of them collapses. He doesn't seem to be breathing and his eyes are glazed. The other guy takes out his phone and calls the emergency services. He gasps, 'My friend is dead! What can I do?' The operator says, 'Calm down. First, let's make sure he's dead.' There is silence, then a gunshot is heard. Back on the phone, the guy says, 'OK, now what?'

In the story about the hunter, we expect the hunter to check his friend's pulse or breathing. But when he shoots his friend instead, the brain reacts to the unexpected outcome by triggering laughter. Bet you didn't know laughing was so complicated!

The part of the brain that understands why a joke is funny is called the prefrontal cortex. People who damage this part of the brain sometimes lose their

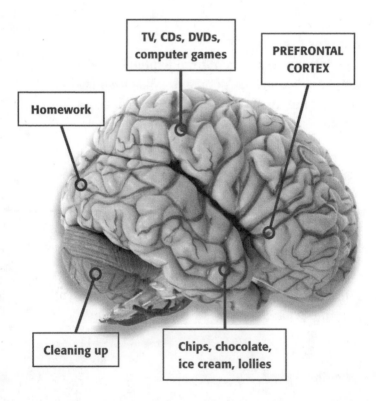

TV, CDs, DVDs, computer games

PREFRONTAL CORTEX

Homework

Cleaning up

Chips, chocolate, ice cream, lollies

sense of humour. When my friend John was diagnosed with a brain tumour, his wife Jane noticed that he couldn't understand puns or double meanings any more. Jane had to be careful what she said because John couldn't tell when she was joking.

WHO PUT THE PUNCH IN PUNCHLINE?

The end of a joke is called the punchline. It's a phrase that's been around since the early 1920s. Television hadn't been invented then, and people enjoyed vaudeville shows which were full of wisecracks and pranks. Jokes were often acted out by two performers, a 'funny man' and a 'straight man'. The funny man played pranks on the straight man, who was always serious, no matter what was going on. At the end of a gag, the funny man pretended to punch the straight man, which made the joke even funnier for the audience.

this better be funny!!

One reviewer called this part of the joke the 'punchline' and the saying seems to have stuck.

WHO PUT THE PUN IN PUNCH?

The secret of joke-writing is knowing where to start. And guess what – it's not at the beginning! The best way to make up a joke is to know how it ends. If you can figure out a good punchline, you're nearly there.

Punchlines hold the key to great gags for another reason. See the first three letters? P-U-N means a play on words that sound or look the same. Take 'sail' and 'sale' for example: the words sound the same but have different meanings. That makes them ideal for getting a giggle – or a groan! Here's an example:

Q: When is the best time to buy a yacht?
A: When it's on sale.

Luckily, the world is full of words that sound the same but have different meanings. Once you start noticing them, you'll really start to see the punny side of life!

JOKES THAT FALL FLAT

Telling jokes is all about timing. If people feel happy, they'll probably laugh out loud. If they feel sad, a joke could cheer them up. But if they feel angry, it might be best to wait until they've cooled down.

If you think a joke is funny, chances are that other people in your age group will find it funny too. Younger people may not understand it. Older people may find it silly. You'll need to experiment to see which jokes appeal to which age groups.

2
KNOCK-OUTS AND SiDE-SPLiTS

Knock-knock jokes are often the first jokes we understand as young children. Knock-knock jokes follow a pattern, so they are easy to remember:

Knock knock
Who's there?
Snow.
Snow who?
Snow time for jokes – just open the door!

Knock knock
Who's there?
Shirley.
Shirley who?
Shirley you recognise your
own mother!

WHY iS iT FUNNY?

These knock-knock jokes work because the name of
the person knocking at the door sounds like another
word. 'Shirley' sounds like 'Surely' and 'Snow' sounds
like 'It's no'.

As with all jokes, the key is in the punchline.
You expect to hear someone's name when you ask,
'Who's there?' But your mind is tricked and the name
you hear turns out to have a different meaning.
The punchline should also be something that might
be said in a doorway. For example, if the end of the
second joke was, 'Surely you like custard', it wouldn't be
as funny.

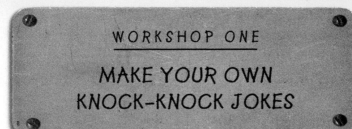

MAKE YOUR OWN
KNOCK-KNOCK JOKES

Write a list of names
on a piece of scrap paper.

Here
are
some
ideas:

- **People you know**
- **Names in magazines
  or newspapers**
- **Names from TV programs**

Take another piece of paper.
Head it up at the top like this:

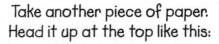

Look at your list of names. Say each name to
yourself. When you find a name that sounds
like another word, write the name in List A.
Write the word it sounds like in List B.

12

LIST A

Lena
Willy
Carrie
Noah
Jonah

LIST B

lean a
will he
carry
know a
do you own a

All knock-knock jokes follow this pattern:

Knock knock
Who's there?

_____

_____ who?

PUNCHLINE

Use one of your names from List A
to fill in the gaps.

When you get to the punchline,
find a funny ending for the List B word or phrase.
For example the 'Jonah' joke might end:

**'Jonah red sports car?
Better run, it's rolling down the hill.'**

Use the lists to make up more jokes.

You can also use surnames, cities, countries,
animals and food in List A.

STILL KNOCKING

Knock knock
Who's there?
Albert.
Albert who?
Albert a million bucks you can't guess
who's knocking.

Knock knock
Who's there?
Daryl.
Daryl who?
Daryl be trouble if you don't open dis door soon.

Knock knock
Who's there?
Kenya.
Kenya who?
Kenya *please* open the door?

Knock knock
Who's there?
Venice.
Venice who?
Venice dis door going to be opened?

SIDE-SPLITS

Now that you've warmed up with some knock-knock jokes, let's try some side-splits. Here are two examples:

Q: What part of a window hurts the most?
A: The window pane.

Q: What card game do you play in hospital?
A: Patience.

WHY IS IT FUNNY?

Side-splits are jokes that use puns or words with double meanings to get a laugh. In these examples, the puns are 'pane' and 'pain' and 'patience' and 'patients'. The question in a side-split always gives clues to the answer. The word 'hurt' is the clue in the first joke and 'card game' is the clue in the second joke.

Luckily, the English language is full of words which sound the same but have different meanings. You can even write several jokes using the same pair of words!

MAKE YOUR OWN SIDE-SPLIT JOKES

Use a dictionary to find words that sound
the same but have different meanings.
(The spelling can be the same or different.)
Choose three words that have several meanings.
Call this 'List A'.

For example:

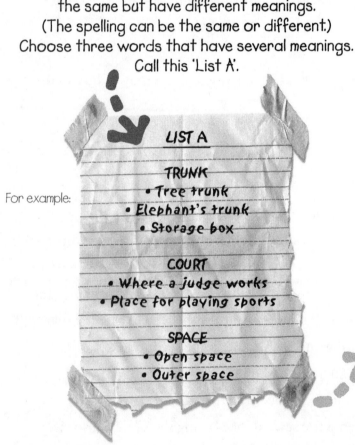

LIST A

TRUNK
• Tree trunk
• Elephant's trunk
• Storage box

COURT
• Where a judge works
• Place for playing sports

SPACE
• Open space
• Outer space

Look at each set of words you have chosen.
Try to find a way of linking two of the
meanings with a question.

Some words will easily make jokes.
Others will take time. If you get stuck,
choose another set of words.

Here are
three examples
using words
from List A:

Q: Where does an elephant
store his belongings?
A: In his trunk.

Q: Where do they send bad
basketball players?
A: To court.

Q: Why did the astronaut move
to a bigger house?
A: He wanted more space.

I tink imb
doin do
sneeze

SIDE-SPLITTERS

Q: What do you eat while you're driving?
A: Traffic jam.

Q: How do you keep a cat quiet?
A: Push the paws.

Q: Why didn't the chicken have a job?
A: Because she kept getting laid off.

Q: Why couldn't the piece of wood find anything to do?
A: Because he was a little board.

I hate chicken jokes!

Q: Why didn't the man take any money to the public pool?
A: Because he wanted to swim free style.

Q: What part of a book is the happiest?
A: The contents.

Q: When does a golfer pick his nose?
A: After he gets a bogey.

3

LAUGHERS LAST LONGER

Have you heard that 'laughter is the best medicine'? No one's quite sure who said it first, but it may come from this old Bible verse: 'A merry heart does good like a medicine, but a broken spirit dries the bones'.

And it's true! As well as giving your muscles a workout, laughter triggers chemicals that make you feel good, stay alert, remember more and feel creative. What's more, your brain can't tell the difference between real and fake laughter – so your body can benefit even if you have nothing to smile about. Try chuckling anyway!

19

THE COMICAL CURE
OF NORMAN COUSINS

American journalist Norman Cousins was diagnosed
with a life-threatening disease in 1964. His time in
hospital seemed to add to his problems, so he checked
himself out of hospital and into a hotel. Believing that
stress had caused his illness, Cousins watched funny
movies and television programs including the Marx
Brothers and *Candid Camera*. He also took high doses
of vitamin C.

The treatment worked and Norman Cousins slowly
recovered. He wrote about his experiences in a book
called *Anatomy of an Illness*. Norman Cousins lived
many more years and eventually died after a heart
attack in 1990, aged 75.

A CHUCKLE A DAY CAN ...

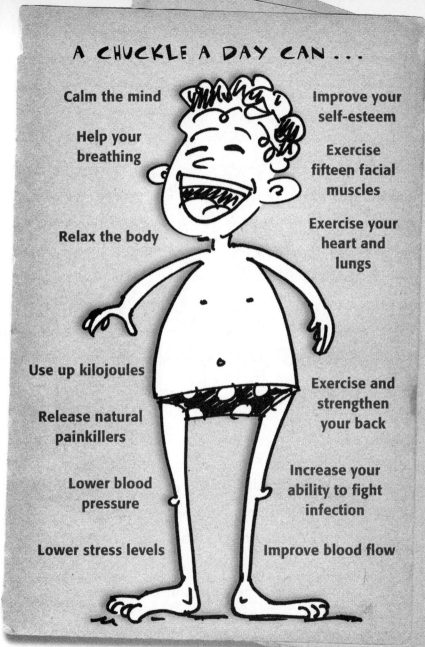

Calm the mind

Improve your self-esteem

Help your breathing

Exercise fifteen facial muscles

Relax the body

Exercise your heart and lungs

Use up kilojoules

Exercise and strengthen your back

Release natural painkillers

Lower blood pressure

Increase your ability to fight infection

Lower stress levels

Improve blood flow

Many ancient cultures knew that laughter could help sick people. One South American rainforest tribe held laughter festivals to help sick people recover more quickly. And centuries ago in Asia, doctors were known to encourage their patients to laugh when things weren't going well.

GETTING THE GiGGLES

Like yawning, laughter can be catching. Researchers have discovered that the brain has a special detector which reacts to laughter. When we hear someone else giggling, the detector triggers other parts of our brain so that we giggle too.

That's why laugh tracks or 'canned' laughter are used on TV comedy shows. Laugh tracks were first used to help radio comedians perform without a live audience. The idea was first used on a TV program in 1950, on *The Hank McCune Show*. There was no live audience so the producers played a laugh track after each joke to encourage viewers at home to enjoy the show.

In 1962, a laughter epidemic in Tanzania that started at a girls' boarding house lasted for six months. A joke between three girls soon spread to more than half of the school. Fits of laughter lasted from minutes to hours. Teachers tried to stop the epidemic by closing the school, but that caused it to spread through villages and other schools until 1000 people were giggling in bursts. Eventually isolating the villages and schools from each other ended the laughter outbreak. Some researchers think high levels of stress may have caused a sort of mass hysteria that spread from group to group.

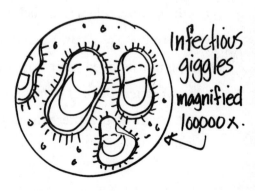

Infectious giggles magnified 100,000x.

In 1995, Dr Madan Kataria was researching an article on the health benefits of laughter when he woke up one morning with the idea of starting a laughter club. If it was so good for you, he thought, why not get more people chuckling? He started a small club in India and told jokes for the first few meetings. When he ran out of good gags, Dr Kataria taught yoga and breathing techniques to get people laughing. The idea has proved so popular that it has spread to more than 2500 laughter clubs throughout the world.

In 1998 the first World Laughter Day was held. This day is now celebrated each year on the first Sunday in May. In 2000 on World Laughter Day in Denmark, 8200 people laughed their way into the Danish pages of the *Guinness Book of World Records* for the most people laughing together without reason.

WHY DO WE LAUGH?

Researchers have suggested three different theories to explain why we laugh. The first is called the Superiority Theory and suggests that we laugh at things that make us feel better than other people. It explains why we laugh when someone gets a pie in the face or makes a mistake.

The second theory is the Incongruity Theory. That's when we see two things that don't normally go together and we laugh as a way of dealing with the strangeness of the situation. An example of this is when a toddler wears his underpants on his head.

The last theory is the Relief Theory. It says that people laugh to release tension and to relax – for example when we watch a funny movie. This theory also explains why some people laugh when they're nervous or frightened. It's a way of coping with tension. Laughing can separate us from tricky situations and help us avoid stress.

iT'S A GAS

For most people, going to the dentist is no laughing matter. One thing that can help ease the pain is laughing gas. Laughing gas is really nitrous oxide, which is a mild anaesthetic.

Laughing gas was discovered by an English scientist named Joseph Priestley in 1772. He thought the gas would work as a preservative, but his experiments failed. Another Englishman, Humphrey Davy, experimented with the gas a little more and watched the way people reacted

oh yesh, zhat's hirarious!.

in amusing ways after inhaling it. It made them do silly things such as swaying and falling over, which made other people laugh. That's how it got the name 'laughing gas'. It was used for 40 years as sideshow entertainment at carnivals and fairs. One day a dentist called Horace Wells noticed that one of the participants had been injured but hadn't felt any pain. The rest is history.

Laughing gas is still used by some dentists today, and women sometimes use it to ease the pain of childbirth.

4

GO CRAZY

Are you crazy about sports? You can certainly go crazy writing jokes about every sport you can think of! And if laughing is so good for us, then laughing about sports must be the best exercise ever.

Q: Which piece of sports equipment makes the most noise?
A: A racquet.

Q: What game do you play if you leave your boots at home?
A: Sock-er.

WHY iS iT FUNNY?

Most people play or watch sports, so they'll probably understand the puns you use in sports jokes.

In the first joke on this page, the words 'racquet' and 'racket' sound the same, but one means a long-handled bat used for hitting a ball while the other means a loud noise.

The second joke is a bit different. Socks and soccer don't sound or look exactly the same, but they are close enough to make the joke funny.

WORKSHOP THREE

MAKE YOUR OWN SPORTS JOKES

Think of a sport you know well
because you play or watch it often.

List all the words you can think of that
are used in that sport. Call this 'List A'.

Here's an
example for
soccer:

LIST A

- Ball
- Shoot
- Dribble

Some of the words in List A may have
two meanings. They may also sound like another
word with a different meaning. For example:
'court' and 'caught'. Start a 'List B'
and write down any different meanings
for the sporting words in List A.
Use a dictionary if you need some help.

30

For example:

LIST A
• Ball
• Shoot
• Dribble

LIST B
• Formal dance
• New plant, or something you do with a gun
• What a baby does with its saliva

Choose one of your word pairs from List A and B.

Think of a way to link the meanings.
Use the two meanings to write a joke.

Here are two examples using **shoot** and **dribble**:

Q: Why was the soccer player sent to jail?
A: For shooting.

Q: Why do babies make good soccer players?
A: They're great at dribbling.

This flow chart also works
for hobbies that use special words
e.g. computers, music, cooking or animals.

MORE SPORTING MOMENTS

Q: What kind of jewellery do gymnasts prefer?
A: Rings.

Q: Why wasn't the chicken allowed to play basketball?
A: Because there were no fouls allowed.

Yet another chicken joke

Q: What did the baseball fan give his girlfriend for her birthday?
A: A diamond.

Q: What do basketball players do with their biscuits?
A: Dunk them.

Q: How did the tennis ball become a squash ball?
A: It sat on the road.

Q: How old do you have to be to play tennis?
A: Tennish.

JUST PLAIN CRAZY

You may not be mad about sports. But you may be mad! Here is a joke-writing workshop for those of you who like to try something a little wild.

Q: What is yellow and speeds?
A: A banana in a racing car.

looks appealing a

Q: What has stripes and good table manners?
A: A zebra in a restaurant.

WHY IS IT FUNNY?

Sometimes it's good to throw in a crazy joke every now and again – especially when your listeners aren't expecting it. Crazy jokes don't follow any of the rules we've been talking about. Crazy jokes put two different things together in a way that makes the punchline so bizarre that it's funny. With these jokes, you can let your imagination run wild. Why not try making some up yourself? They're easy and fun to write.

MAKE YOUR OWN CRAZY JOKES

Make a list of animals and food – try two of each to start with. Call this 'List A'.

For example:

LIST A
Pig
Frog
Cake
Strawberry

Now write a list of four places you can go or things you can do. Call this 'List B'.

For example:

LIST B
Drinking a milkshake
Riding a bike
Swimming lessons
Parachuting

Think of a word or phrase to describe each word or phrase in Lists A and B. Call these new lists C and D.

For example:

LIST A
Pig
Frog
Cake
Strawberry

LIST C
pink
green
covered in icing
red

LIST B
Drinking a milkshake
Riding a bike
Swimming lessons
Parachuting

LIST D
burping
two wheels
wet
floating

The pattern for these jokes is:
'What is _____ and _____?

Fill in the gaps with a word from
List C and a word or phrase from List D.
Combine the corresponding List A and B words
to form the punchline.

For example:

Q: What is pink and burps?
A: A pig drinking a milkshake.

Q: What is wet and covered in icing?
A: A cake taking swimming lessons.

CRAZY CACKLES

Q: What is white and furry and wears a leotard?
A: A polar bear on a trapeze.

Q: What is yellow and wears a tie?
A: A lemon in his best clothes.

Q: What weighs four tonnes and is good at balancing?
A: An elephant at the top of a flagpole.

Q: What has 100 legs and pointy toes?
A: A centipede doing ballet.

Q: What has a long neck that goes up and down?
A: A giraffe on a trampoline.

Q: What is yellow and goes downhill fast?
A: A banana on a water slide.

Q: What is striped and lays eggs?
A: A chicken in jail.

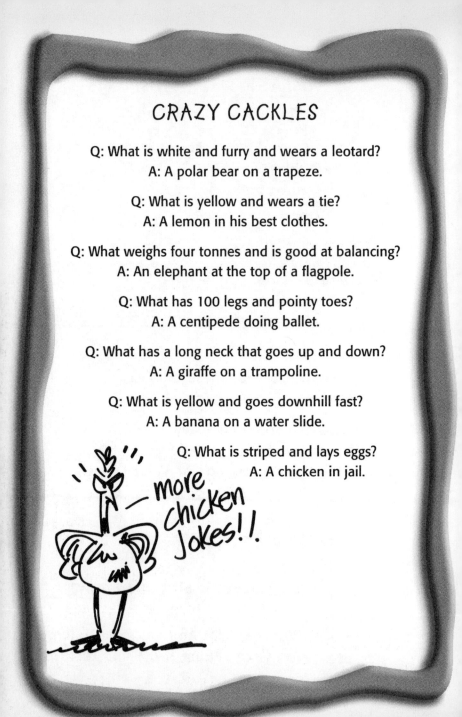

more chicken jokes!!

5

CLOWNING AROUND

If you had a good sense of humour in the Middle Ages – and there probably wasn't much to laugh about in those days – you might have been given the job of court jester.

Most kings kept jesters in their courts. Jesters dressed in brightly coloured coats and leggings called motley. The jester's hood was sometimes decorated to look like the head of a donkey or a rooster. Bells were attached to his costume, his hood and his long pointed shoes. He told jokes, played pranks and made amusing comments to help the courtiers forget about their worries for a while.

I feel stupid!

NOT SO FOOLISH

Jesters were sometimes called court fools, but most of them were clever and some gave the king good advice.

Jesters often used humour to sort out differences between those around them. One famous French jester named Jehan was called in to sort out a problem between a baker and a porter. The baker was angry because the porter was sniffing his food. He thought the porter should have to pay for each sniff. Jehan the jester pretended to agree with the baker, then asked the porter to rattle the coins in his pocket. He told the baker that the sound of the coins paid for the smell of the food.

William the Conqueror, who lived from about 1027 to 1087, had a jester named Gollet who saved his life. Gollet heard of a conspiracy against William and ran to his master's bedroom door, beating against it with an iron hammer and crying out until William awoke.

JESTERS IN BATTLE

Triboulet was a jester who served the French king in the 1500s. The king liked to take his jester into battle with him, but Triboulet wasn't very brave. He hid under the bed whenever he heard the sound of a cannon. This annoyed one nobleman so much that he threatened to kill the jester. The king assured Triboulet that if that happened, he would certainly kill the nobleman half an hour later. Triboulet replied, 'Couldn't you execute him half an hour before?'

KiNGS, QUEENS AND JOKERS

The joker in a pack of cards looks a lot like a royal court jester. But packs of cards haven't always had jokers. The joker is an 'extra' which was first introduced in America in about 1863 and England around 1880. It was invented by players of a game called euchre (pronounced 'yuker') who wanted an extra trump, or winning, card in the pack.

A MOTLEY CREW

Jesters were common in Europe, Great Britain, Japan, Russia, Africa, Persia and India. The Chinese emperor first employed jesters 4000 years ago. Jesters in the Chinese court could say whatever they liked, and in 300 BCE one jester managed to stop the emperor's plans to have the Great Wall of China painted with lacquer. Thousands of workers had died during the building of the wall as the work was so dangerous.

Thousands more would have died if it had been painted. The jester joked about how long the project would take and the emperor finally gave up the idea.

Jesters went out of fashion in China after about the seventeenth century. They became unpopular in Europe and Britain about 100 years later, but there were still some jesters in Scotland in the 1800s.

SEND iN THE CLoWNS

Just as jesters joked with kings and courtiers, clowns cheered up crowds of ordinary folk. But unlike jesters, most clowns don't tell jokes. They make us laugh by their silly clothes and foolish behaviour. They teach us to see the funny side and stop taking life too seriously.

Clowns have existed in most cultures throughout history. In Ancient Greece, clowns performed on stage after a serious drama, as an antidote to the tragedy of the play. They acted out a funny version and made all the heroes look like fools. Ancient Romans also used clowns in their plays. One character, known as Stupidus, always made mistakes. The other actors would pretend to get annoyed, knocking him around the stage to the delight of the audience.

When the Roman emperor became a Christian, he closed down the theatres. Clowns started travelling around from town to town to make their living, performing with musicians, acrobats and jugglers. There were no stages, so the clowns had to clear a space for the performance. Using a balloon on a stick, they hit people to keep them out of the performance area. Sometimes a clown would carry a broom and sweep people out of the way if they got too close to the actors.

William Shakespeare was the first playwright to use clowns as real actors. He hoped they would make his tragedies more dramatic.

Two clowns employed in Shakespeare's troupe were Will Kemp and Richard Cowley. They didn't always do as Shakespeare asked, or say the words that he had written for them.

Instead, they would dance a jig whenever they felt like it or make up their own lines. Shakespeare was annoyed by these antics – but the audience loved it.

CLOWN BABY

Imagine working in the circus from the age of two! That's what happened to Joey Grimaldi. By 1798, when he turned twenty, Joey was an experienced acrobat and performer and is remembered as one of the world's most famous clowns. Joey's life was tough. His tumbling often left him with broken bones and – even though he was good at making other people laugh – he was sometimes sad. One day when he felt really down, he visited a doctor. The doctor couldn't find anything physically wrong with the man so he recommended that his patient cheer himself up by going to watch the great Grimaldi perform. You can imagine his surprise when Joey admitted that he was Grimaldi!

Germany's Clown

Till Eulenspiegel was a clown who travelled throughout Germany playing tricks on people. In one town he promised to paint a mural on a bare wall. The finished wall was still bare, but the clown explained it had magical qualities. Only those with no secrets to hide could see the mural's beauty. Of course, no one wanted to admit they couldn't see anything, so everyone admired the wall. The clown left town before people realised the truth.

A Clown in Rome

Philemon was a clown in Ancient Roman times. He is now known as St Philemon because he died for his faith. In those days, Romans believed they had to please the gods by sacrificing food, money and animals. The Christians didn't believe in the Roman gods and, if they refused to make a sacrifice, they were put to death.

One day a Christian asked Philemon to impersonate him and pretend to make a sacrifice at the temple.

At first Philemon thought it would be a great joke and agreed to do it. But when he got to the temple, he couldn't bring himself to pretend. Philemon admitted to the guards that he was a Christian. He was such a popular clown that the people didn't want him put to death. But Philemon refused to change his mind and died for his Christian beliefs.

CLOWNING AROUND THE WORLD

Several cultures throughout history have used clowns in healing rituals. Ceremonial clowns in native American tribes dressed up in strange clothing and acted the fool to get sick people laughing again. Medicine men in ancient African tribes danced in special costumes to drive out the evil forces that they believed were responsible for sickness in the community.

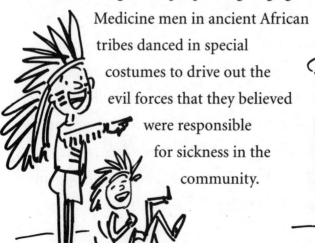

In eastern Asia, clowns often took part in serious plays and ceremonies. While the actors playing royal characters used ornamental umbrellas called parasols, the clowns followed along carrying their parasols upside down and falling over each other.

The Australian Murngin tribe uses a clown to stop tribal members from fighting. If a fight breaks out, the clown starts to imitate the quarrel, using exaggerated movements. This distracts the fighters and gets them to see the funny side of their argument. (This sometimes works in the schoolyard too!)

DOCTOR CLOWN

In recent years, clowns have found a regular place in some hospitals. One of the first people to bring humour into modern hospitals was Dr Hunter Adams, known as Patch Adams. A movie starring Robin Williams tells the story of how Patch was inspired to become a doctor through his own experiences in hospital. He used his clowning skills to help patients make a speedy recovery.

Clowning is now used in many hospitals around the world to help take away the stress of illness, particularly for sick children and elderly people. Professional clowns use juggling, mime, magic and jokes and 'do their rounds' dressed in funny hats and red noses, carrying rubber chickens instead of stethoscopes. Some doctors and nurses also dress up like clowns when they visit their patients, because they believe so strongly in the healing power of humour.

This won't hurt a bit.

rubber chicken soup

6

SAY WHAT?

Making up words is great fun. Once you get the hang of it, you might even start a trend.

Q: What ballet move do you perform in your sleep?
A: A pillowette.

Q: What is the tastiest building in the world?
A: The Trifle Tower.

WHY IS IT FUNNY?

'Say what?' jokes are funny because they change the sound of a familiar word. The real ballet move is called a pirouette. By asking the right question and changing the sound slightly, you have a joke that connects two seemingly unconnected things – ballet and sleep!

In the second joke, 'trifle tower' rhymes with France's well-known Eiffel Tower. That's the key to 'say what?' jokes: make sure the sound of the made-up word is close enough to the sound of the real word for your listeners to make a connection straight away.

SAY THAT AGAIN?

Q: What do mermaids have on toast?
A: Mermalade.

Q: What do you call a rude plane?
A: A swearaplane.

Q: What do you call a hippo with chicken pox?
A: A hippospotamus.

Q: How does a magician drink his tea?
A: From a cup and sorcerer.

Q: Where do bees go on Saturday nights?
A: A stingalong.

MAKE YOUR OWN 'SAY WHAT?' JOKES

Think of some interesting words with three or more
syllables: food, musical instruments, animals, items
of clothing, or anything else you like the sound of.
If you're having trouble, use a dictionary.

Write down four or five words. Call this 'List A'.

For example:

LIST A
Merry-go-round
Saxophone
Alligator
Dictionary

Try to find a good rhyming word for the first one
or two syllables of each word. Call this 'List B'.

For example:

LIST B
Merry rhymes with SCARY
Sax rhymes with SNACKS
Alli rhymes with SMELLY (almost!)
Diction rhymes with FICTION

Write a new list of made-up words
using the rhyming words. Call this 'List C'.

For example:

LIST C

Scary-go-round
Snaxophone
Smellygator
Fictionary

These new words are the punchlines for your jokes.

Link the real meaning of the List A words
with the meaning of the List B words
to make a joke.

Here
are some
examples:

Q: Which fairground ride is the
most frightening?
A: The scary-go-round.

Q: Which musical instrument is the tastiest?
A: The snaxophone.

Q: What do you call an alligator
with bad breath?
A: A smellygator.

Q: How do you find out the meanings
of made-up words?
A: Look them up in a fictionary.

TWiSTiNG TiME

The jokes in the next workshop are similar to the ones on the previous pages. The only difference is that – instead of being made-up words – the punchlines in these jokes are real words with a new twist.

Q: What do you call a cow that is always sulking?
A: Moo-dy.

Q: What do you call the place where a UFO crashes?
A: Astroturf.

WHY iS iT FUNNY?

Remember the first rule of joke writing? Start at the end.

The punchline in twister jokes is a word which has been given a new twist. All you need to do is find an interesting word and give it a new meaning.

In the first joke on this page, the word 'moody' starts with the sound made by a cow – MOO! In jokes like this, you need to make use of the true meaning of the whole word – moody – and the word contained within it – moo. So the joke has to be about a cow and a bad mood.

Tell her an udder joke

Compound words are also great for using in jokes because you can combine two meanings. A compound word is made up of two other words – like 'pitch/fork' or 'water/melon'. In the second joke, 'astroturf' is artificial grass, but it is given a new meaning, made up of 'astro' (outer space) and 'turf' (the stuff under our feet).

Let's try some of our own.

MAKE YOUR OWN
TWISTING JOKES

Write down a list of compound words, or other
words that have more than one meaning.
Call this 'List A'.

For example:

LIST A
- Toadstool
- Lollipop
- Humble

These words are the punchlines for your new jokes.

Now, separate the words in each
compound word. Write the meaning,
or meanings, of each word.
Call this 'List B'.

For example:

LIST B

Toad	Frog
Stool	Chair
Lolly	Sweet for children
Pop	Modern music
	Soft drink
Hum	Not singing
ble	Bull

The pattern for these jokes is:

'What do you call _____?'

The words in List A form the punchline.
Find a way to link the meanings of your List B
words to create the joke.

Here
are some
examples:

Q: What do you call the place
a frog sits to eat breakfast?
A: A toadstool.

Q: What do you call sweet music?
A: Lollipop.

Q: What do you call a bull who won't sing?
A: Humble.

KEEP TWISTING

Q: What do you call a librarian who lives underground?
A: A bookworm.

Q: What do you call a baby chicken you buy
at a garage sale?
A: Cheap.

Q: What do you call a pig with a skin problem?
A: Hogwarts.

Q: What's the best place to store pork?
A: A piggy bank.

Q: What do you call a group of people
waiting to play pool?
A: A cue.

7

FOOLS AND TRICKSTERS

What's that green stuff coming out of your nose?
Ha, fooled again!

When you play a trick on someone, it's called a
practical joke. Most practical jokes are harmless, but
some can be dangerous. It's okay to put a whoopee
cushion on someone's chair, but it's not safe to pull
someone's chair out when they're about to sit down.
Practical jokes usually make the joker feel great, but
the victim feels embarrassed at being fooled. If you're
a practical joker, watch out! Some of your victims
might want revenge!

APRIL FOOLS!

There's one day in the year when people expect to be tricked. The first day of April is known as April Fools' Day in many countries around the  world. No one knows who made the first April Fools' Day joke, but the idea may have started around 1582.

Long ago, 1 April was the first day of the European year. In 1582 Pope Gregory XIII introduced a new calendar, called the Gregorian Calendar, which we still use today. The new calendar changed New Year's Day to 1 January, but news travelled slowly. People who didn't realise were called 'April fools' and other people played practical jokes on them. It wasn't long before 1 April was known throughout France, England and Scotland as a day for playing pranks such as sending people on fake errands, tying shoelaces together and giving silly gifts.

French victims of 1 April pranks are called '*poissons d'avril*' which means 'April fish'. The name relates to how easy it is to catch newly hatched fish in April.

French children take the joke further by taping pictures of fish to their friends' backs.

Scottish people prefer to attach 'kick me' signs to people's backs. They call 1 April 'Taily Day' and jokes played on that day are all about backsides.

Sometimes TV and radio stations play tricks on the public on April Fools' Day. One BBC program convinced people that spaghetti grew on trees. Another tricked people into thinking that gravity would lessen on that day, meaning they could jump higher than usual – and even float around like astronauts!

FOOLS OF THE WORLD UNITE

Many cultures have other special days set aside for playing pranks on people. Spanish and Mexican people try to outwit each other on 28 December, a sad date in history when many children were killed, but now a day of joy and fun. Portuguese people celebrate a special day before Lent when they throw flour at each other. India's special pranks day is part of the spring festival when they play tricks on each other and paint their faces with bright colours. On 13 April children in Thailand throw water at their friends as part of a festival celebrating the Thai New Year.

HOAXES

Hoaxes are pranks that fool large numbers of people. History records many famous hoaxes, some of which have lasted for a long time. In the early 1900s, two English girls aged ten and sixteen tricked the world with photos of 'real' fairies. When they were old women, they finally admitted the photos were of paper cut-out fairies standing on hatpins!

Hugh Troy was an American university student in the 1920s who loved hoaxes. He found a rubbish bin made out of a real rhinoceros foot. One snowy night he and a friend filled the bin with weights and suspended it on lines between them. They walked around the university campus with the rhino foot making prints in the snow. Next morning, other students discovered the prints leading to a hole in an ice-covered lake. Because the lake was connected to the university's drinking supply, half of the people there stopped drinking tap water. The other half thought the water tasted of rhinoceros!

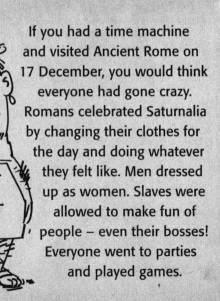

If you had a time machine and visited Ancient Rome on 17 December, you would think everyone had gone crazy. Romans celebrated Saturnalia by changing their clothes for the day and doing whatever they felt like. Men dressed up as women. Slaves were allowed to make fun of people – even their bosses! Everyone went to parties and played games.

8

ALL MIXED UP

**Q: What do you get when you cross
a spider with an elephant?
A: Daddy-long-nose.**

**Q: What do you get when you
cross a monkey with a flower?
A: A chimpansy.**

WHY IS IT FUNNY?

The jokes on this page mix things that don't usually go
together: a spider and an elephant, or a monkey and
a flower. The punchline in mixed-up jokes can be a

made-up word like daddy-long-nose, or it can be a real word with a different spelling, like chimpansy.

You can have a lot of fun with mixed-up jokes!

MIXED-UP MADNESS

Q: What do you get when you cross
a cow with Aotearoa?
A: Moo Zealand.

Q: What do you get when you cross
pasta with a question?
A: Spaguessi.

Q: What do you get when you cross
a rabbit with a garden hose?
A: Hare spray.

Q: What do you get when you cross
a giant gorilla with a skunk?
A: King pong.

Q: What do you get when you cross
a joke with a skeleton?
A: A funny bone.

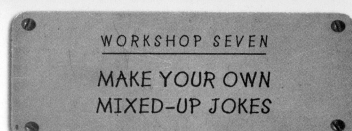

MAKE YOUR OWN MIXED-UP JOKES

Make a list of animals, places, sayings, flowers and food. It's best to use compound words or longer phrases such as the ones below. Call this 'List A'.

For example:

LIST A

Baked beans
Great Britain
Peanut butter

Write a describing word for each word you have found. Call this 'List B'.

For example:

LIST B

Tasty snack
Country – United Kingdom
Sandwich spread

Choose one part of each word
in List A and find a rhyme for it.
Call this 'List C'.

For example:

LIST C

Baked Queens
Grate Britain
Peanut flutter

These words are the punchlines for your new jokes.

Look at your List C words. Think about how
they have changed from your List A words.
Write a describing phrase for that change.
Call this 'List D'.

For example:

LIST D

Queens – royalty
Grate – cheese
Flutter – butterfly

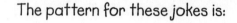

The pattern for these jokes is:

'What do you get when you cross a _____ with a _____?'

Use the words in Lists B and D to fill in the gaps. The words in List C form the punchline.

Here are some examples:

Q: What do you get when you cross a tasty snack with royalty?
A: Baked queens.

Q: What do you get when you cross the United Kingdom with cheese?
A: Grate Britain.

Q: What do you get when you cross a sandwich spread with a butterfly?
A: Peanut flutter.

I knew I shouldn't have had beans for breakfast

THE MISSING LINK

Q: Why is a magician like a cricket player?
A: They both like doing hat tricks.

Q: Why is a coat like a marathon runner?
A: They both get worn out.

WHY IS IT FUNNY?

Missing-link jokes use double meanings to link two very different things and give them something in common.

As usual, these jokes start with a good punchline. A 'hat trick' is a cricketing term meaning bowling three batsmen out in a row. But hat tricks for magicians are something very different.

In the second joke, the phrase 'worn out' means one thing to a marathon runner and something else when it is used to describe a piece of clothing.

Ideas for these kinds of jokes are all around you – on TV, in books, at school – so listen well and keep a notebook and pencil handy!

MAKE YOUR OWN MISSING-LINK JOKES

Write a list of words or phrases
that have more than one meaning.
This is 'List A'.

Here's an
example:

LIST A

- Trunk
- Ring
- Bee

These words are the punchlines for your new jokes.

Look at each of the words in List A.
For each word, write two things
that are connected with that word.
Call this 'List B'.

LIST B

TRUNK	RING	BEE
Elephant	Circus clown	Flower
Tree	Finger	A, B, C

For example:

The pattern for these jokes is:

'Why is a _____ like a _____?'

Use the List B words to fill the gaps in the question.
The punchline starts with 'They both _____.'

Use the words in List A to complete the joke.

Here are some examples:

Q: Why is an elephant like a tree?
A: They both have long trunks.

Q: Why is a circus clown like a finger?
A: They both look good in a ring.

Q: Why is a flower like the letter A?
A: A bee always comes after it.

STILL MISSING

Q: Why is a manicurist like a secretary?
A: They both do filing.

Q: Why is a battery like a burglar?
A: They both get charged.

Q: Why is a chicken like a broken toilet?
A: They're both fowl.

Q: Why is a postcard like a rugby player who breaks the rules?
A: They both get sent off.

Q: Why is a newspaper like a tomato?
A: They're both red.

Q: Why is a pile of dirty dishes like a good basketball player?
A: No one likes to see them sitting on the bench.

9

TONGUE TWISTERS

Have you ever noticed how funny the English language is? If you get your tongue stuck when you're saying one word, another completely different word can pop out. When that happens, it's best to laugh along with the people who've heard your mistake. Some people have even become famous for making a mess of the English language.

i Hit My Bunny Phone

In the late 1800s and early 1900s a man named William Archibald Spooner worked at England's Oxford University. Spooner became famous for getting his words mixed up. Instead of saying 'lighting a fire', he would say 'fighting a liar'. And instead of telling a lazy student that he had 'wasted two terms', he said the young man had 'tasted two worms'. Today, if you make a similar mistake, it's called a spoonerism.

See if you can figure out what these spoonerisms really mean . . .

- Go and shake a tower.
- May I sew you to another sheet?
- That's a lack of pies!
- You have mad banners.
- Bred any good rooks lately?

— What about forkerisms?

A PIGMENT OF YOUR IMAGINATION

Richard Sheridan wrote plays in the 1700s. One of his plays, *The Rivals*, featured a character called Mrs Malaprop who used big words but often got them wrong. Instead of saying something was the 'pinnacle of politeness' she called it the 'pineapple of politeness'. Today, slips of the tongue are still called malapropisms. Here are five malapropisms. See if you can find out what the speaker really meant to say instead of:

- ☼ I got stuck in the **revolting** doors.
- ☼ Flying saucers are an optical **conclusion**.
- ☼ The flood damage was so bad they had to **evaporate** the city.
- ☼ He used a fire **distinguisher** to put out the flames.
- ☼ She starts on one subject then goes off on a **tandem**.

OXYMORONIC

If you listen closely when people speak, you'll notice some strange word choices. Ever described someone as 'pretty ugly'? Pretty and ugly are opposites – yet we use phrases like that all the time. Another example is 'seriously funny'. They're called oxymorons – which is a seriously funny word in itself! Here are some more interesting oxymorons for you to think about:

- burning cold
- original copy
- almost exactly
- inside out

PICKLED PEPPERS

Ever been tongue-tied? Maybe someone asked you to repeat a tongue twister.

Most people have heard of Peter Piper. He's the guy who picked a peck of pickled peppers. (Say it really fast: *Peter Piper picked a peck of pickled peppers.*)

Tongue twisters are sentences that repeat the same starting sound and are tricky to get your tongue around. It's easy to say a tongue twister slowly. But the faster you get and the more often you say it, the more likely you are to get mixed up – sometimes with hilarious results! The more you practise, the better you'll get at tongue twisters. In fact, 'practice makes perfect' works as its own tongue twister: try it and see!

Do you sometimes have trouble finding exactly the right word? That's because there are so many to choose from. There are more than a million words in the English language and hundreds more are added each year. Perhaps that's why it's so easy to make a slip of the tongue. It's hard for our brains to keep up with it all!

Here's another funny tongue twister:

A skunk sat on a stump
And thunk the stump stunk
But the stump thought the skunk stunk.

RiDDLE ME THiS

There was once a green house. Inside the green house was
a white house. Inside the white house was a red house.
Inside the red house were lots of babies.

This is an ancient word play called a riddle. Did you
work it out? The answer is a **watermelon**.

Riddles have been around for thousands of years,
but early riddles weren't always funny. Sometimes they
were so serious that answering correctly was a matter
of life or death.

One of the oldest and most famous is the riddle
of the Sphinx, a legendary winged monster which
tormented the Theban people of Ancient Greece.
The Sphinx killed everyone who couldn't answer its

riddle. Finally, a hero named Oedipus solved the riddle and the Sphinx killed itself. Let's see how well you would have done if you met the Sphinx:

What goes on four legs in the morning, two legs in the daytime and three legs in the evening?

(Turn to page 88 for the answer.)

Here are some riddles for you to try out on your friends. Or you could make up some new ones of your own.

Q: I give away my first letter. I give away my second letter. I give away all my letters. Who am I?

A: A postman.

Q: What is as light as air but can't be held for long?

A: Your breath.

Q: What gets lost every time you stand up?

A: Your lap.

10
THE LAST LAUGH

I hope you've enjoyed writing jokes, reading jokes and learning about laughter. Remember to keep smiling, laugh a lot and see the funny side of life. It really helps! And, to send you on your way, here are some of my favourite jokes to share with your friends.

Q: Why couldn't the egg finish telling jokes?
A: He kept cracking up.

Q: Why did the man sleep under the car?
A: He wanted to wake up oily in the morning.

Knock knock
Who's there?
Mr Bean.
Mr Bean who?
Mr Bean standing here
for 10 minutes already.

Just wait there for the time bean.

Q: What did the auctioneer say when he sold
the pair of cymbals?
A: Going, going, gong.

Q: What did the mother say when her son
got pins and needles?
A: Good. You can fix the buttons on this shirt.

Q: Why was the alien looking for a gardening job?
A: He had green fingers.

Q: Where do you
take sick horses?
A: Horsepital.

feeling ok? Nay!

Knock knock
Who's there?
Ya.
Ya who?
Keep the noise
down, will you?

Q: What did the astrologer say to the vampire?
A: Let me write your horrorscope.

Q: What do dogs do when they agree on something?
A: Shake on it.

Knock knock
Who's there?
Otter.
Otter who?
Otter brush your hair before you
open the door next time.

Q: What kind of dog carries a disease?
A: Bac-terrier.

Q: What do you call a girl
with a sweet tooth?
A: Candy.

Knock knock
Who's there?
Royal.
Royal who?
Royal be round later.
I'm Tim.

Q: Why didn't the oyster have any friends?
A: He was too shellfish.

Knock knock
Who's there?
Chicken.
Chicken who?
Chicken side and
see if I left my
keys on the table,
will you?

Q: Why did the truck driver stop for a meal?

A: Because he came to a fork in the road.

Q: What card game do crocodiles play?

A: Snap.

Get the cards and make it snappy!

Q: Why did the barber leave his job?

A: He'd had too many close shaves.

Q: Why was the dog's surprise party ruined?

A: Because someone let the cat out of the bag.

Q: What did the coach say to the player who kept complaining that his boots were too big?

A: Put a sock in it.

Q: Why did the worm lose the court case?

A: He didn't have a leg to stand on.

He was legless your Honour!

Q: What did the number three say to the number four?
A: I'll get even with you if it's the last thing I do.

Q: Why did the boy smash all the clocks
in the morning?
A: His mother told him to kill some time
before school.

Q: What do you get when you cross a large animal
with perfume?
A: A smellyphant.

Q: Where do umpires hold their meetings?
A: The Umpire State Building.

Q: Why did
the chicken lay
an egg?
A: So the pig
didn't have to.

Arrgh! Another terrible chicken joke!!!

SHARON HOLT was born in Auckland, the eldest and bossiest of four daughters. Her goal in life was always to be an author, but on the way she worked as a teacher and a journalist and ran a children's bookshop. For fun, Sharon navigated in car rallies, learned to fly planes, delivered singing telegrams and visited South America.

Sharon lives in Kihikihi, New Zealand, with her husband and two children.

ROSS KINNAIRD loves jokes. This got him into trouble at school. Now his ability at maths is truly funny. He lives in Auckland and when he is not busy drawing funny pictures, he is usually found crossing the road to get to the other side. He is emperor, president and sole member of the International League of Chicken Jokers.

(Please note that all hate mail from chickens will be passed on to the proper authorities . . . he does not find this amusing.)

THANKS

The willing helpers at the Te Awamutu Public Library – headed by the fabulous Sheree – have made my research job so much easier. Thanks for that.

I am also thankful to the children and teachers at Puahue School and Korakonui School who helped by trying out the flow charts in this book. Some of the jokes are evidence of their creativity.

The contributions of Eva Mills and Sarah Brenan at Allen & Unwin have been outstanding. Thank you both for being so encouraging and supportive – not to mention your ability to magically turn too many words into just the right amount.

Thanks also go to my family and friends for understanding why I had to spend so long at the computer.

And thanks to Ross for bringing my jokes to life with his cartoons.

Sharon Holt

The publishers would like to thank istockphoto.com and the photographers named for images appearing on the following pages: Matt Knannlein (metal plate); Stefan Klein (taped paper and old paper); Cornelia Shaible, pages i and 37 (fool's sceptre); Mark Evans, page 6 (model of human brain); Nancy Louie, pages 26 and 27 (plastic teeth); Hendrik Frank, page 40 (joker card); Bruce Lonngren, page 47 (rubber chicken).

This will do it! ─

WiTTY WoRDS oF WiSDoM

I am thankful for laughter, except when milk comes out of my nose. WOODY ALLEN

Laughter is the shortest distance between two people. VICTOR BORGE

Seven days without laughter make one weak. JOEL GOODMAN

Laughter is an instant vacation. MILTON BERLE

A good time for laughing is when you can. JESSAMYN WEST

Laughter is the sun that drives winter from the human face. VICTOR HUGO

A clown is like aspirin, only he works twice as fast. GROUCHO MARX

At the height of laughter, the universe is flung into a kaleidoscope of new possibilities. JEAN HOUSTON

Funny is an attitude. FLIP WILSON

He who laughs, lasts. MARY PETTIBONE POOLE

Laughter is a tranquilliser with no side effects. ARNOLD GLASGOW

Laughter is part of the human survival kit. DAVID NATHAN

Where To Find Out More

Books

Duncan Ball, *Selby's Side-Splitting Joke Book*, Angus and Robertson, Sydney, 2002

George Beal, *The Superbook of Word Games*, Kingfisher, London, 1986

Carol Crowther, *Clowns and Clowning*, Macdonald Educational, London, 1978

Andy Jones, *The Enormous Book of Hot Jokes for Cool Kids*, ABC Books, Sydney, 2004

Tim Trewartha, *Laugh-a-Licious Jokes for Kids*, Ibis Publishing, Melbourne, 2004

Alan Trussell-Cullen, *Playing with Words*, Shortland Publications, Auckland, 1999

Websites

- www.holistic-online.com/Humor_Therapy/humor_therapy.htm
- www.patchadams.org
- www.rxlaughter.org
- www.fun-with-words.com
- www.coai.org/history.htm
- www.psy.vanderbilt.edu/faculty/bachorowski/laugh.htm

For teachers

Patch Adams with Maureen Mylander, *Gesundheit!*, Healing Arts Press, Vermont, 1998

Richard Baines (ed.), *Journey through Humour*, Oxford University Press, Oxford, 2003

Lisa Bany-Winters, *Funny Bones*, Chicago Review Press, Chicago, 2002

Simon Critchley, *On Humour (Thinking in Action)*, Taylor & Francis, London, 2002

Brad Schreiber, *What Are You Laughing At?: How to Write Funny Screenplays, Stories and More*, Michael Wiese Productions, Seattle, 2003

INDEX

A: The answer to the riddle of the Sphinx is man. He crawls on four legs as an infant, walks on two legs as an adult and uses a walking stick (a third leg) in his old age.